Anatomy of an EARTHQUAKE

by Renée C. Rebman

Consultant:
Dr. Kent M. Syverson
Professor of Geology
University of Wisconsin-Eau Claire

CAPSTONE PRESS
a capstone imprint

Velocity is published by Capstone Press,
1710 Roe Crest Drive, North Mankato, Minnesota 56003.
www.capstonepub.com

Library of Congress Cataloging-in-Publication Data
Rebman, Renée C., 1961–
  Anatomy of an earthquake / by Renée C. Rebman.
     p. cm. — (Velocity. Disasters)
  Summary: "Describes the science of earthquakes, including their prediction and
effects"—Provided by publisher.
  Includes bibliographical references and index.
  ISBN 978-1-4296-4797-7 (library binding)
  ISBN 978-1-4296-7363-1 (paperback)
  1. Earthquakes—Juvenile literature. I. Title. II. Series.
  QE521.3.R43 2011
  551.22—dc22   2010004159

Editorial Credits
Mandy Robbins, editor; Heidi Thompson, designer; Svetlana Zhurkin, media researcher;
Eric Manske, production specialist

Photo Credits
Alamy: The Print Collector, 8 (bottom); Capstone Press, 8–9 (top and middle), 13 (top), 16
(top), 17 (top), 28–29, 35 (top), 41 (bottom); Dreamstime: Oriontrail, cover (top), Secondshot,
45 (right); Eric Hoffmann, 10, 11 (top); Getty Images: AFP/Daniel Garcia, cover (bottom),
AFP/Odd Andersen, 42, National Geographic/James P. Blair, 12, National Geographic/
Winfield Parks, 32–33; iStockphoto: Baris Simsek, 6–7, Bart van den Dikkenberg, 11 (bottom),
Eric Foltz, 29 (top), Feng Yu, 26 (middle), Ivan Dinev, 16, Jackie DesJarlais, 45 (left), Jonathan
Maddock, 26 (bottom), Rui Pestana, 39, Sarah Holmstrom, 17; Library of Congress, 22
(bottom), 29 (bottom), 30; Newscom: 37, MCT/San Jose Mercury News/Tom Van Dyke, 31
(top), Sipa Press/Rony Zakaria, 4–5, Ubaldo Gonzalez, 38, WENN, 25, Xinhua/David de la
Paz, 36 (bottom), Yuan Man, 41 (top); NOAA/LCDR Mark Wetzler, NOAA Ship Fairweather,
23 (bottom); Photo courtesy of EarthScope, a program of the U.S. National Science
Foundation, 20–21; Shutterstock: A.S. Zain, 34–35, artlali, 14 (bottom), 15, C. Michael Neely,
13 (bottom), Dale A. Stork, 40, Dariusz Kantorski, 27, Darren J. Bradley, 14 (top), Jonathan
Feinstein, 31 (bottom), joyfull, 44, Melica, 36 (top), Nikonov (metal background), throughout,
Oculo (mosaic design element), cover and throughout, Restyler, 26 (top), Robert Paul Van
Beets, 42–43, Sebastian Kaulitzki (scratched metal background), back cover and throughout,
Stanislav E. Petrov (cement background), throughout; Visuals Unlimited: Inga Spence, 18,
Science VU/NGDC, 24–25, Science VU/NGDC–NOAA, 22–23 (back)

TABLE OF CONTENTS

SUDDEN CHAOS

It is late in the afternoon on September 30, 2009. Shoppers crowd the markets in the city of Padang in western Indonesia. School children study at their desks. Office workers look forward to ending their day. Suddenly, the ground begins to shake violently. Buildings twist and collapse. People run screaming into the streets. An earthquake has struck!

In moments, electricity is cut off in parts of the city, and fires break out. Survivors wander the streets searching for loved ones. Cries of the injured fill the air.

The deadly three-minute quake measured 7.6 on the Richter scale. Dozens of aftershocks follow. Thousands of people are trapped beneath toppled buildings.

Richter scale—a scale that helps scientists measure the energy released during an earthquake
aftershock—a small earthquake that follows a larger one

Off the coast, the earthquake triggers a large **tsunami**. Waves over 20 feet (6 meters) tall pound small coastal villages. The damage and loss of life is massive.

An earthquake is a release of energy when the ground snaps along a fault. Thousands of quakes occur each day, all over the world. Most cause little damage. But the few large ones can be devastating. Each earthquake reminds us that our world is in a constant state of change.

tsunami—a series of waves caused by an underwater earthquake or landslide

fault—a break in the brittle top layer of the Earth where rocks slide past each other

Chapter 1

OUR MOVING EARTH

The Earth seems constant and sturdy. It appears to be made of hard rock and dirt. But the Earth is alive with motion. It is structured in a series of layers.

LOWER MANTLE

OUTER CORE

UPPER MANTLE

INNER CORE

CRUST

The crust is at the Earth's surface. It is 5 to 30 miles (8 to 48 kilometers) deep.

The next layer is called the mantle. The mantle is about 1,800 miles (2,900 km) deep. It has two main sections. The upper mantle is rocky. Together the upper mantle and the crust are called the lithosphere. Earthquakes are caused by movement in the lithosphere.

The lower mantle is more like a soft plastic material. This material is constantly on the move. It heats up, rises toward the surface, and then cools. As it cools, it becomes more dense. Then the matter sinks down, and the cycle begins again. This movement is known as convection.

CONVECTION

Convection is easy to understand. Think of macaroni boiling in a pot of water. The macaroni bubbles to the top of the water. There it cools off and drops back down to the bottom. The macaroni does this in a continuous circular motion.

An outer core of boiling-hot liquid metal lies beneath the mantle. The outer core is about 1,400 miles (2,253 km) thick.

At the very center of the Earth is a solid inner core. It is about 800 miles (1,288 km) thick. This core is hotter than the surface of the sun.

dense—when an object is heavy for its size

Tectonic Plates

Tectonic plates are part of the lithosphere. They are also called lithospheric plates. The lithosphere is 6 to 62 miles (10 to 100 km) deep. There are two kinds of lithosphere.

OCEANIC LITHOSPHERE

Oceanic lithosphere exists deep under the sea.

PERMIAN PERIOD

225 million years ago

TRIASSIC PERIOD

200 million years ago

Wegener's Theory

Alfred Wegener suggested the theory of continental drift in 1912. He thought the edges of the plates could fit together like puzzle pieces. Similar rock types and fossils were found on different continents that seemed to fit together. These continents are now separated by oceans. Wegener thought this proved that all land was once connected.

Scientists threw out the continental drift theory because Wegener didn't know what caused the continents to move. Today scientists know that convection within Earth's layers causes the plates to move.

The continental lithosphere is associated with the **continents**.

ASTHENOSPHERE
The plates float on top of the asthenosphere. This part of the mantle is made of hot rock that acts like plastic. The floating plates move about 4 inches (10 centimeters) each year.

JURASSIC PERIOD
135 million years ago

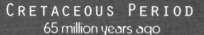

CRETACEOUS PERIOD
65 million years ago

PRESENT DAY

Plate Tectonics

In the 1960s scientists revisited the theory of continental drift. Using new information discovered about the ocean floor, scientists developed the theory of plate tectonics. According to this theory, the Earth's land once formed one giant mass called Pangaea. Pangaea means "all land" in Greek. Due to convection within the Earth, Pangaea began breaking apart 200 million years ago. The tectonic plates eventually moved to form the seven continents we know today. Earthquakes often occur at plate boundaries where tectonic plates meet.

continent—one of Earth's seven large land masses

Convergent Plate Boundaries

Earthquakes at convergent plate boundaries reach **magnitudes** of 9 or more.

Mountain ranges are formed by convergent movement.

Plates collide at convergent plate boundaries.

Convergent movement pushes rock up. This movement forms a ridge as one plate is forced under the other plate.

Divergent Plate Boundaries

When plates spread apart they form a divergent plate boundary. Earthquakes at these boundaries are usually less than a magnitude 8.

Hot liquid rock cools to form new tectonic plates that move apart.

Hot liquid rock pushes up between the tectonic plates.

Transform Plate Boundaries

When plates slide past each other they form a transform plate boundary.

Earthquakes are more likely to occur along these boundaries.

Earthquakes along a transform boundary are usually 8.5 magnitude or less.

EURASIAN PLATE

NORTH AMERICAN PLATE

MID-ATLANTIC RISING

The Mid-Atlantic Ridge is a well-known example of a divergent plate boundary. It runs nearly the entire length of the Atlantic Ocean. The Mid-Atlantic Ridge is formed by the Eurasian Plate and the North American Plate spreading apart.

Iceland lies right on top of the Mid-Atlantic Ridge. The island is slowly being pulled apart. New crust is forming on both sides of the boundary. Someday, the Atlantic Ocean may spill in to fill up the rift. Then Iceland will become two separate islands.

magnitude—the measurement of the amount of energy released by an earthquake

Chapter 2

FINDING FAULT

Earthquakes occur along cracks in the Earth's crust called faults. Faults don't just occur at plate boundaries. They can also exist throughout a tectonic plate.

The constant strain from plate movement produces fault zones. These are areas where the Earth's crust has broken apart. Visible cracks and scarring of the land are present in some fault zones. In others, the breaks are underneath the surface.

SAN ANDREAS
FAULT

Fault Systems

California

HAYWARD
CALAVERAS
SAN ANDREAS
NACIMIENTO
WHITE WOLF
OWENS VALLEY

Pacific Ocean

• Sacramento

GARLOCK
SAN GABRIEL
SIERRA MADRE
MISSION CREEK
BANNING

Los Angeles

NEWPORT-INGLEWOOD
ELSINORE
SAN JACINTO

San Diego

The San Andreas fault in California is the most well-known transform plate boundary in the United States. It is associated with many smaller faults. These connected faults form a fault system.

During a quake, the release of energy from one fault can increase stress on other fault segments. This stress may cause several earthquakes to follow in a short period of time.

FACT: A creeping fault moves slowly. Most creeping faults never build up enough pressure to cause a large earthquake.

SHALLOW EARTHQUAKES

Shallow earthquakes begin close to the Earth's surface. Because the crust is cooler near the surface, shallow earthquakes cause the greatest destruction. To understand why, compare the rock in the Earth to glass.

If you've ever seen someone blowing glass, you know that when the glass is very hot, it will bend. Once it cools, too much pressure will snap or shatter the glass. The rocks in the Earth work the same way. Deep within the Earth, rocks are hotter. They are easier to bend when pressure builds up. This bending action absorbs more pressure. Closer to the surface, rocks are cooler and harder. Instead of bending, they snap. The snapping releases energy in the form of an earthquake.

Stressing Out

All earthquakes are a result of pressure, or stress, being put on rock. It's similar to when you bend a green tree branch. Eventually the stress of bending snaps the branch. But there is more than one type of stress that can cause an earthquake.

Stress can bend layers of rock.

Compressional Stress

In a reverse fault, one side of the earth is pushed up over the other. Reverse faults are a result of compression. Compressional stress causes layers of rock to shorten as though they are being smashed together. This type of stress occurs at convergent plate boundaries.

Imagine smashing a can. As the can is pressed together, the sides get wider. In the end the can is flat. But it's not as narrow as it once was.

Tensional Stress

Normal faults are a result of tension. Tensional stress causes layers of rock to stretch as though they are being pulled apart. Normal faults are found at divergent plate boundaries.

In a normal fault, one side of the earth drops down lower than the other side.

Shear Stress

Shear stress causes rocks to slip past each other. This causes transform faults. The effects of sheer stress can often be seen on the Earth's surface. When blocks of lithosphere shift past each other, the movement can displace fences and roads.

THE CENTER OF THE ACTION

Earthquakes begin underground, usually 12 miles (19 km) or more below the surface. This point is called the focus of the quake. The epicenter is often used to describe the location of a quake. The epicenter is the point on the surface directly above the focus. It refers to a place or city on a map.

Epicenter

12 miles (19 km)

Focus

Making Waves

Earthquakes release energy. This energy moves outward in a series of seismic waves. To better understand earthquake waves, picture what happens when you throw a rock into a pond. As the rock falls to the bottom, the waves move outward in a circle.

Earthquakes release both surface waves and body waves. Surface waves are seismic waves that are trapped near the Earth's surface. They cannot move through the Earth. Surface waves cause the most damage.

seismic wave—a wave of energy caused by an earthquake

P and S Waves

Unlike surface waves, body waves can travel through the Earth. There are two types of body waves. They are primary waves (P waves) and secondary waves (S waves).

P waves are the fastest waves. They can travel 2 to 9 miles (3 to 14.5 km) per second. P waves can travel through solid rock, molten lava, water, and air. P waves move in a straight line, causing a pushing and pulling motion. These waves cause the rumbling sound of an earthquake.

S waves move at about half the speed of P waves. S waves advance with a snakelike movement that causes sideways shaking. These waves cause the ground to shake side-to-side.

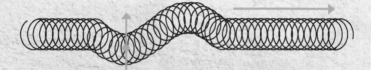

MAKE YOUR OWN WAVES

To understand how P waves and S waves differ, try this experiment. You will need a friend and a slinky.

Stretch the slinky between you and your friend. Now push your end of the slinky forward and quickly pull it back. Notice how a sort of wave moves through the slinky. The wave compresses and stretches the slinky in a straight line. That is how a P wave operates.

Now stretch the slinky between the two of you again. This time, move your hand quickly in an up and down motion. Notice how the wave now moves in a ripple. That is what an S wave does.

Studying Earthquakes

Seismology is the study of earthquakes and seismic waves. Scientists called seismologists have created some amazing tools to help them study earthquakes.

A seismometer measures the strength, duration, and frequency of waves. It even measures tremors that are too small to feel. Seismometers are set up underground where activity is known to occur. Scientists monitor their recordings.

Seismometers consist of two parts. The seismograph detects the strength of the waves. It also tracks how much time passes between waves. Measuring the time difference between the arrival of P and S waves can determine the epicenter.

The second part of the seismometer is the seismogram. It is the actual output of the seismometer. This information is stored on a computer disk. A seismogram looks like a squiggly line. Each spike in the line shows how intense a wave was. It also shows how far apart in time waves occurred.

SEISMOMETER

frequency—the number of times something happens
tremor—a shaking or trembling movement

Richter Scale

Earthquake strength, or magnitude, can be described using the Richter scale. Charles Richter invented this scale in the 1930s. It was based on seismogram recordings.

The Richter scale is structured on the value of 32. The higher the number, the stronger the quake. A small change in the Richter scale represents a huge difference in earthquake energy. Each jump in number means 32 times more energy is released.

Largest earthquake ever recorded was 9.5.

9.5

offshore Chile, 1960
9.5

Alaska, 1964
9.2

Sumatra, 2004
9.1

GREAT

New Madrid
Fault Line, 1812
8

8

There is great devastation and many fatalities possible.

MAJOR

Haiti, 2010
7.2

San Francisco, 1989
7.1

7

STRONG

Damage begins but fatalities are rare.

6

MODERATE

5

SMALL

4

3

2

MINOR

-1   0   1

NOT FELT

Mercalli Scale

The Mercalli scale is numbered from one to 12. The numbers are represented as Roman numerals. This scale measures the amount of damage done by an earthquake. Higher magnitudes don't always cause the most damage. A high-magnitude earthquake in an unpopulated area causes less damage than one in a city.

Chapter 3

PREDICTION & PREPARATION

Predicting earthquakes can save lives and avoid heartbreaking tragedy. Modern science has made some progress in this area. Scientists use two main methods when trying to predict future earthquakes.

The first method is to study the history of earthquakes in particular areas. Large tremors usually happen in patterns. Knowing these patterns can help people predict and prepare for future earthquakes.

SAN FRANCISCO'S PATTERN

In the San Francisco Bay area of California, scientists have noted a pattern. Earthquakes tend to happen in clusters. In the late 1800s, the area experienced several small earthquakes.

In 1906 a very large one hit. It had a magnitude of 7.8. Over the last few decades, this pattern has begun to repeat itself.

In 1989 San Francisco experienced a 7.1 magnitude earthquake. Scientists are unsure if this was the large quake they were expecting or if there is another one yet to come.

Seismic Tools

Scientists also have tools that measure pressure building up in rocks. These tools help scientists determine when a quake may happen.

Strainmeters measure small changes in rock shape over a long period of time. Changes may indicate that pressure is building in the rock.

Installing a strainmeter requires heavy-duty drilling.

Tiltmeters measure changes in slope. They note where the land is either rising or settling. These changes indicate the ground is shifting. Earthquake activity can follow these shifts.

Making a Difference

Hundreds of organizations study earthquakes. One of the best known is the National Earthquake Information Center (NEIC) in Golden, Colorado. The NEIC gathers data 24 hours a day about earthquakes as they happen around the world.

When an earthquake occurs, the NEIC immediately sends the data to federal and state governments. The organization also notifies response teams, media, and other scientists. When a damaging quake happens in a foreign country, the information is passed to that country's American embassy.

Scientists study earthquakes to try to help people prepare for earthquakes, such as the devastating San Francisco quake of 1906.

Earthquakes greater than magnitude 5 since 1980

Low elevation ⟶ High elevation

The U.S. Geological Survey also studies earthquakes. It posts news about earthquakes as they happen. The organization also posts earthquake hazard maps on its Web site. The colors on a hazard map indicate tectonic movement. Red areas are hot spots for earthquake activity.

LEARNING FROM THE PAST

Many organizations and watch centers are set up after a disaster happens. In 1960 an underwater earthquake off the coast of Chile triggered a tsunami. The huge waves caused massive destruction in Chile. They also killed people in Hawaii and Japan.

Soon the United States established a Pacific Ocean tsunami warning system to warn people of possible tsunamis. There are dozens of tsunami watch centers in the Pacific. They share information with the hundreds of earthquake-watching organizations. If an underwater earthquake happens, a tsunami watch can be issued within half an hour. If a tsunami develops, a warning is sent out. It gives people time to leave areas that might be hit.

tsunami warning buoy

Ring of Fire

Some areas of the world are especially prone to earthquakes. The Ring of Fire refers to the edges of the plates around the Pacific Ocean. This area is prone to both earthquakes and volcanic eruptions. The Ring of Fire affects thousands of miles of coastal area. These areas include parts of Asia, North and South America, and Australia.

Red indicates tectonic activity around the Pacific Plate's Ring of Fire.

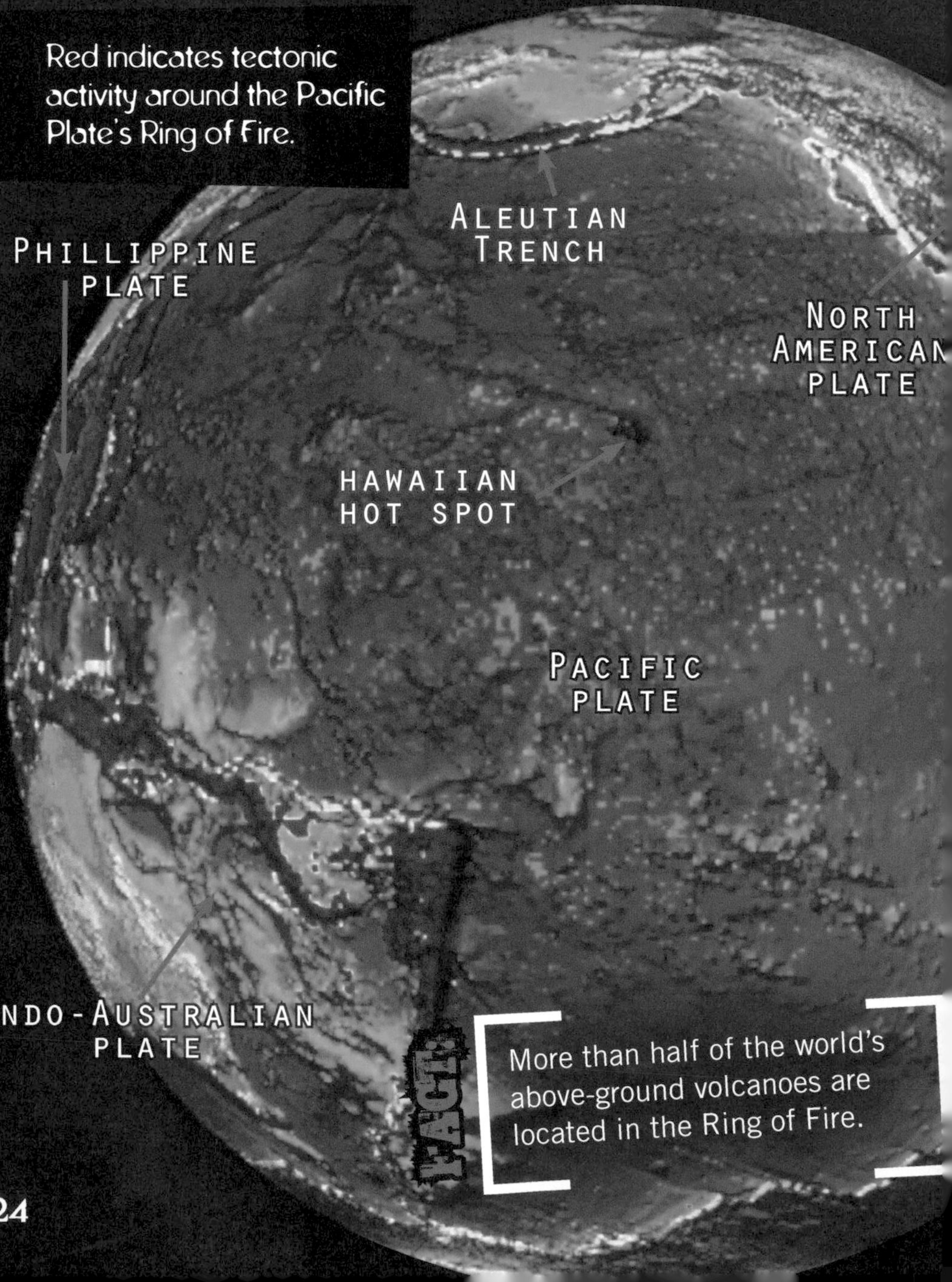

ALEUTIAN TRENCH

PHILLIPPINE PLATE

NORTH AMERICAN PLATE

HAWAIIAN HOT SPOT

PACIFIC PLATE

INDO-AUSTRALIAN PLATE

FACT:
More than half of the world's above-ground volcanoes are located in the Ring of Fire.

The Pacific Plate is sliding into and under other plates. This activity causes the many earthquakes and volcanoes in the Ring of Fire.

Seismologists are extremely interested in the Ring of Fire. Anyone living in these areas is at risk of experiencing an earthquake. Seismic risk maps show the amount of earthquake activity around the ring.

ANIMAL INSTINCTS

Some people think animals can sense when an earthquake will occur. People have reported pets behaving strangely right before an earthquake. Some pets have paced restlessly. Dogs have howled, birds flapped in their cages, and cats ran away.

Some examples occurred before famous quakes. People reported horses acting odd before the 1906 San Francisco earthquake. Before a 1964 Alaskan earthquake, bears came out of hibernation weeks earlier than usual. In 2008 thousands of frogs migrated away from a fault zone in China two days before an earthquake hit the area.

Some scientists think animals might be able to sense small tremors that humans don't feel. Other scientists think animals can smell gases that are released into the air before an earthquake. But most scientists agree that animal behavior is not a reliable predictor of earthquake activity.

In 2008 frogs hopped away from a fault zone before an earthquake in China.

Preparing Yourself

There are steps you can take to make your home safer in an earthquake. Attach heavy shelves and wall hangings securely to the wall with bolts. Bolt bookcases and tall dressers to the wall. Make sure all drawers and cupboard doors latch securely. This will prevent objects from flying out.

You should also prepare an earthquake kit. Your kit should include:

- Flashlight
- Battery-charged radio to listen to earthquake reports
- Cell phone to call for help

- Batteries for flashlight and radio

- Whistle to call for hel if you are trapped

- 1 gallon (3.8 liters) of bottled water per person, per day
- Canned food
- Non-electric can opener
- Face mask to keep from breathing in dust

- First aid kit and any medications regularly needed

FIRST AID

Surviving an Earthquake

Once an earthquake hits, you must act quickly to protect yourself. If you are inside a building, try to get under a piece of sturdy furniture. Doing this will protect you from falling objects. Stay away from mirrors, windows, or glass objects that could shatter. Avoid tall dressers or anything that can fall on you.

If you are outside when an earthquake hits, get away from any buildings or bridges that could fall on you. Move to an open area.

If you are in a moving car, the driver should pull to the side of the road. Cars should be parked away from power lines, trees, or large signs. Wait in the car for the shaking to end.

Chapter 4

MAJOR EARTHQUAKES

Many famous earthquakes stand out in history. Most are memorable because of their high magnitudes. Some caused thousands of deaths and millions of dollars of damage. Earthquakes remind us that devastating changes can occur in minutes.

New Madrid

The New Madrid Fault Zone is named after New Madrid, Missouri. This fault line runs 150 miles (241 km) along part of the Mississippi River.

On December 16, 1811, at 2:15 a.m., an earthquake struck along the fault. Frightened residents of New Madrid ran from their homes. Buildings crumbled around them, and sinkholes opened in the earth. Seismologists believe the quake could have been equal to an 8.1 on the Richter scale.

C A

New Madrid
Fault Zone

New Madrid

Mississippi
River

FACT

Tremors from the New Madrid earthquake rang church bells in Boston, which was 1,058 miles (1,703 km) away!

MEXICO

For months afterward, thousands of aftershocks struck a large portion of the country. The strongest aftershock occurred on February 7, 1812. It was at least a magnitude 8.

A

• Boston

✪ Washington, D.C.

This tremor caused the Mississippi River to run backward for a short while. Much of the land along the river was reshaped. New lakes, like Reelfoot Lake, were created. Landslides caused parts of the shoreline to slide off into the water. River water filled low spots and caused new swamps and lakes to appear.

FACT!

President James Madison felt some of the New Madrid tremors. He was in the White House 900 miles (1,448 km) away.

29

San Francisco Disasters

San Francisco sits over California's San Andreas Fault. The city has been jolted by many earthquakes. Residents have survived two memorable quakes, one in 1906 and another in 1989.

In 1906, 400,000 people lived in San Francisco. Many of the buildings were built of wood and brick. Worse yet, the buildings near Fisherman's Wharf were built on unstable marshland.

The 7.8-magnitude quake caused buildings to topple. The destruction sparked fires that broke out all over the city. Blazing fires burned more than 28,000 buildings. Estimates of the death toll have ranged from 700 to 3,000 people. About 225,000 people were left homeless.

The 1989 quake hit on October 17 at 5:04 p.m. It lasted 15 seconds and registered 7.1 on the Richter scale. Buildings fell and landslides occurred. Fires broke out and burned for three days.

OAKLAND BAY BRIDGE

Devastation was widespread. A section of the Oakland Bay Bridge collapsed, killing one person. An upper section of the Nimitz Freeway also fell and killed 42 people. Many homes throughout the city were declared unsafe and were later demolished. Overall, 63 people died and 3,757 were injured. More than 12,000 people lost their homes.

SAFE AT HOME PLATE

On October 17, 1989, San Francisco hosted the third game of the World Series. The game was set to begin at 5:30 p.m. San Francisco's freeways were usually packed with traffic that time of day. But thousands of people had left work early to go to the game or to watch it on TV. As a result, the freeways were fairly empty. If not for the game, many more lives would have been lost when the bridge and the freeway collapsed.

Alarm in Alaska

A quake registering 9.2 on the Richter scale struck Anchorage, Alaska, on March 27, 1964. It was the largest earthquake to ever hit that state. Tremors were felt on more than 500,000 square miles (1,294,994 sq km) of land.

The earthquake caused damages over an area of 50,000 square miles (129,499 sq km). The massive tremor tore buildings in two. Large cracks appeared in the ground. Part of the waterfront at the Port of Seward slid off into the ocean and changed the coastline.

During the first three days after the quake, almost 300 aftershocks were reported. One tremor lasted four minutes. It was the longest tremor ever recorded.

The epicenter of the Alaska quake was near an inlet on Prince William Sound. The underground tremor set off a tsunami. The small island of Chenega was hit by a 70-foot (21-m) wave. The large wave killed 23 residents. A 40-foot (12-m) wave hit the town of Seward, Alaska. The waves of the tsunami traveled as far as Hawaii and Japan. Combined, the earthquake and tsunami killed more than 130 people.

Alaska is the most earthquake-prone state in the United States. A magnitude 7 earthquake occurs there almost yearly.

Wave of Destruction

On December 26, 2004, an earthquake struck off the coast of the Indonesian Island of Sumatra in the Indian Ocean. The quake occurred along a convergent plate boundary and registered at 9.1 on the Richter scale. It released as much energy as 23,000 atomic bombs. The underwater earthquake created a gigantic tsunami that ripped across the Indian Ocean, devastating 11 countries. It was the deadliest tsunami in recorded history, taking more than 230,000 lives.

Tsunami waves can strike between five minutes and one hour apart. Some people thought it was safe to return to shore after the first wave. They were killed when the second wave struck.

FACT: Before the tsunami hit, hundreds of animals were seen moving to higher ground. Very few animal bodies were found in the aftermath.

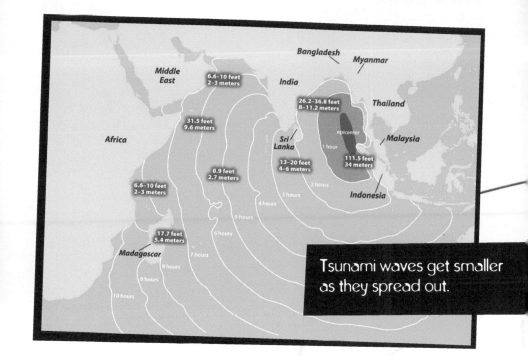

Bangladesh
Myanmar
Middle East
6.6–10 feet 2–3 meters
India
Sri Lanka
26.2–36.8 feet 8–11.2 meters
Thailand
31.5 feet 9.6 meters
epicenter
Malaysia
Africa
1 hour
8.9 feet 2.7 meters
13–20 feet 4–6 meters
111.5 feet 34 meters
6.6–10 feet 2–3 meters
2 hours
Indonesia
3 hours
4 hours
5 hours
17.7 feet 5.4 meters
6 hours
Madagascar
7 hours
8 hours
9 hours
10 hours

Tsunami waves get smaller as they spread out.

When the gigantic waves retreated, many people died being sucked out to sea. Boats were stranded, and fish were left to die in the sand. After the ocean returned to normal, thousands of bodies washed ashore.

The tsunami was as high as 111.5 feet (34 m) in some places. Survivors said the deadly ocean waters sounded like a jet engine.

Disaster in Haiti

CUBA

North America Plate

HAITI

DOMINICAN REPUBLIC

Port-au-Prince

Caribbean Plate

* EPICENTER
● CITY
\ FAULT LINE

On January 12, 2010, a magnitude 7 earthquake devastated the poverty-stricken nation of Haiti.

Haiti shares the island of Hispaniola with the Dominican Republic. Hispaniola is located where the North American Plate and the Caribbean Plate meet.

The earthquake occurred along a transform plate boundary between the two plates.

FACT

One lucky survivor was pulled from the rubble after being trapped 16 days.

The epicenter was close to the city of Port-au-Prince. The ground beneath the city is thick **sediment**, the worst type of material for withstanding tremors. Between the thick sediment, poor building codes, and cheaply built structures, many buildings toppled. Around 200,000 people were killed. Thousands more were injured. Most residents of Port-au-Prince were left homeless.

aftermath in Port-au-Prince

Many Haitians tried to dig out loved ones trapped in crumbled buildings. But they lacked large equipment to move the rubble.

A week after the initial earthquake, a 6.1-magnitude aftershock hit. The tremor caused even more damage and slowed rescue efforts.

sediment—bits of loose sand, clay, or small rock

Chapter 5

THE AFTERMATH

After a strong earthquake, cities are in chaos. Fires break out. Landslides and avalanches can occur. Broken gas and water lines pose serious dangers to citizens. Damaged roads and bridges may prevent rescue and medical workers from helping victims.

Once aid workers reach earthquake victims, they face other problems. Hospitals and fire stations may be damaged and unsafe for use. Finding safe shelters for injured people is a difficult task.

Earthquake Drills

In many earthquake-prone regions, cities and schools have regular earthquake drills. These drills teach citizens and rescue staff what to do during and after an earthquake. Citizens are taught how to determine which buildings are safe. They learn how to deal with ruptured pipes, gas lines, and downed electrical wires. Rescue and medical workers practice treating injured people. Volunteers act like injured victims. Workers also practice coordinating communication and search-and-rescue teams.

An earthquake in the Sichuan province of China devastated the city of Yingxiu. More than half of the residents were killed.

aftermath in Yingxiu, China

Rescue Work

The aftermath of an earthquake can be frightening. Searching for victims is a dangerous task. Rescue workers must work quickly, yet safely. They face the risk of buildings collapsing. They also need to be careful not to disturb rubble.

Trained rescue teams use different methods to find trapped earthquake victims. One method uses thermal imaging cameras. A thermal imaging camera locates people by detecting body heat.

THERMAL IMAGING CAMERA

Another device, a trapped-person detector, picks up vibrations. It is helpful when trapped people bang on walls or pipes to attract attention. What is not easily heard by people is picked up on the detector.

Rescue teams also use highly trained dogs to sniff out trapped victims.

TRAGEDY IN TANGSHAN

On July 28, 1976, a 7.8-magnitude earthquake hit Tangshan, China. Tremors rarely happened there. No one was prepared. Homes came crumbling down. Mining tunnels collapsed, causing huge sinkholes. A hospital and a train sank into the holes.

Survivors and rescue workers scrambled to dig out those who were trapped. But a major aftershock hit 15 hours later. Many of the rescue workers and most of the people still trapped were killed. More than 240,000 people died as a combined result of the quake and the aftershock.

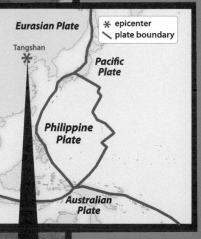

Eurasian Plate

Tangshan

⁎ epicenter
\ plate boundary

Pacific Plate

Philippine Plate

Australian Plate

The Tangshan earthquake took residents by surprise because the city lies within the Eurasian Plate. It is not located near a known fault line. Scientists are still unsure what caused the quake.

Damage Assessment

Structures closest to the epicenter often suffer the worst damage. But this is not always the case. How buildings are built and what they are built on have a great impact on destruction as well.

Sturdy wood–framed houses may survive the initial quake. But fires often break out after an earthquake. Entire sections of a city may go up in flames.

Brick and stone structures seem strong. But tremors can crack the mortar holding them together. The cracks may cause entire buildings to topple.

UP TO CODE

Cities with poor building codes or none at all suffer the most during earthquakes. In 2003 a quake in Bam, Iran, killed 30,000 people. Bam's building code had been updated in 1989, but many standing structures had been built before then.

A quake of similar strength struck southern California that same year. Only two lives were lost. The California government spends billions of dollars constructing buildings and bridges that can better withstand quakes.

aftermath in Bam, Iran

What a structure is built on is also important. A house built on solid rock is much safer than a house built on thick, weak sediment.

Sediment acts like Jell-O during an earthquake. It will continue to shake, or jiggle, long after the initial tremor. This shaking can cause great damage.

Smart Construction

Today many buildings in earthquake-prone areas are constructed to withstand very strong quakes. One of the best ways is to create buildings with rigid steel framing. The first floor and the foundation must provide strength. There must be enough load-bearing walls and columns to support all floors built above them.

A steel grid at the foundation can keep a structure level. The first floor must be securely bolted into the foundation at numerous points.

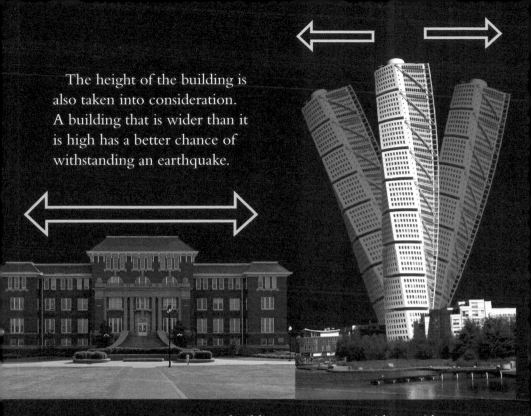

The height of the building is also taken into consideration. A building that is wider than it is high has a better chance of withstanding an earthquake.

Large tremors cause buildings to sway in a side-to-side motion. Buildings that are top-heavy or built on unstable ground are the most likely to topple over.

Code Improvements

Scientists place monitoring devices on public buildings and structures in earthquake-prone areas. By studying data, scientists can see how these structures react during large tremors. Based on this information, improvements in building standards can be suggested.

Earthquakes are a reminder of the shifting forces of the Earth. These forces are as amazing as they are dangerous. Scientists are constantly working to minimize the danger and save lives. Perhaps some day they will be able to predict earthquakes more accurately. Until then, preparing for these natural disasters is the smartest thing to do.

GLOSSARY

aftershock (AF-tur-shok)—a small earthquake that follows a larger one

continent (KAHN-tuh-nuhnt)—one of Earth's seven large land masses

dense (DENSS)—when an object is heavy for its size; density is the amount of matter in a specific volume

epicenter (EP-uh-sent-ur)—the point on the Earth's surface directly above the place where snapping causes an earthquake

fault (FAWLT)—a break in Earth's lithosphere where rocks slide past each other

frequency (FREE-kwuhn-see)—how often something happens

magnitude (MAG-nuh-tood)—a measure of the amount of energy released by an earthquake

Mercalli scale (mer-CAL-ee SKALE)—a scale based on the damage done by an earthquake

Richter scale (RIK-tuhr SKALE)—a scale that helps scientists measure the energy released during an earthquake

sediment (SED-uh-muhnt)—bits of loose sand, clay, or small rock

seismic wave (SIZE-mik WAYV)—a wave of energy caused by an earthquake

tectonic plate (tek-TAHN-ik PLATE)—a large section of the Earth's crust and upper mantle; also called a lithospheric plate

tremor (TREM-ur)—a shaking or trembling movement

tsunami (tsoo-NAH-mee)—a series of waves caused by an underwater earthquake or landslide

READ MORE

Aronin, Miriam. *Earthquake in Haiti.* Code Red. New York: Bearport Pub., 2011.

Dwyer, Helen. *Earthquakes.* Eyewitness Disaster. New York: Marshall Cavendish Benchmark, 2010.

Fradin, Judy, and Dennis Fradin. *Earthquakes: Witness to Disaster.* Witness to Disaster. Washington D.C.: National Geographic Society, 2008.

McLeish, Ewan. *Earthquakes in Action.* Natural Disasters in Action. New York: Rosen Pub. Group, 2009.

Montgomery, Heather. *How to Survive an Earthquake.* Prepare to Survive. Mankato, Minn.: Capstone Press, 2009.

INTERNET SITES

FactHound offers a safe, fun way to find Internet sites related to this book. All of the sites on FactHound have been researched by our staff.

Here's all you do:

Visit *www.facthound.com*

Type in this code: 9781429647977

INDEX